Dear World, Congratulations! The book you are holding in your hands is infected with the infectious poetry of Charlotte Seley. Your temperature will rise. Your brain will wrinkle. Your palpitations will palpitate. Seley breaks her heart to break yours. She is "jealous / of the states you live in / the orange slices you share / the words we don't have..." World, read Seley. Get ill and "Expand your palette & ride out the whispering blue wind."

>   Peter Jay Shippy
>   Author of *A Spell of Songs* and
>   *How to Build the Ghost in Your Attic*

The poems in Charlotte Seley's *The World Is My Rival* strike as quickly and brightly as lightning and illuminate not only the landscape but the interiors of buildings and the private lives of those within. I dare anyone to find a poet with more linguistic energy and insight. I am thrilled for all who have waited for this book, and for those who won't know what hit them when they read it.

>   John Skoyles
>   Author of *Suddenly It's Evening: Selected Poems*
>   and *Inside Job*

I'm writing you from the event horizon of the whole world. It's somewhere inside Charlotte Seley's poems. What happened was, I read *The World is My Rival*, and the book, a body into which grief and celestial ennui have drilled, pulled itself into its own hole. That is, her book swallowed itself, and I went with it. Charlotte Seley stayed behind, lamenting the inability of the human mind to correlate all its contents. She wants to see everything at the same time: the angora sweater she is wearing and also the angora rabbit before it molted. She maintains that her map is not the territory, but you will follow it anyway, all the way to Beard Island, where the bewhiskered beloved lives, even as Seley warns you: "love/is unoriginal/when it's me and I'm making it." Her jealousy however is intense and wholly (holy) original. She wants every cell that her body has ever sloughed off, every other possible life, mode, and thought--and those of her lover's. She is driving herself out of her mind. Which thankfully makes more room for us there.

>   Darcie Dennigan
>   Author of *Animal Land* and
>   *Palace of Subatomic Bliss*

The World is My Rival

Charlotte Seley

SPUYTEN DUYVIL
NEW YORK CITY

ACKNOWLEDGEMENTS

Barrelhouse: "Chill," "spoiled in six ways," "For Ivan Who Dreams of Elsewhere," and "With Change Machine and Pearls"

H_NGM_N: "I Am Not Fluent in Any Languages," "The World is My Rival," "My Body is What Ails Me," and "Elegy"

InDigest Magazine: "His Legends Were Like Unicorns"

inter|rupture: "no bulls in the china cabinet" and "Homewrecking is different from housebroken"

The Knicknackery: "Beard Island, Population 1" and "The White Diamonds are a Necklace of Feathers"

LEVELER: "Rock Salt"

Luna Luna Magazine: "All of Us Are Disappearing All the Time"

METAZEN: "I Was Born a Shrieking Slot Machine and "Carousel of Iridescence"

Passages North: "Pity Us Poor Devils"

Rattle: "Bright Red Bit"

summer stock: Earlier versions of "Free to be without," "From a supermarket," and "The Triangle"

Vinyl Poetry: An earlier version of "Majestic Blues"

© 2018 Charlotte Seley
ISBN 978-1-947980-49-5

Library of Congress Cataloging-in-Publication Data

Names: Seley, Charlotte, author.
Title: The world is my rival / Charlotte Seley.
Description: New York City : Spuyten Duyvil, [2018]
Identifiers: LCCN 2018018750 | ISBN 9781947980495
Classification: LCC PS3619.E4627 A6 2018 | DDC 811/.6--dc23
LC record available at https://lccn.loc.gov/2018018750

"The world is in fact just that: an obligation to share. The world (the worldly) is my rival." — Roland Barthes

I Am Not Fluent in Any Languages

The second I scream underwater,
        I care less about this wreck.
Constellations of bubbles erupt water and the alphabet
        breaks into cameos—I have much delight
when it returns to me, when I can make it

work in ways I didn't know it knew how.

        I am not fluent in any languages.

Like when I said to throw a penny at an oncoming train and let it lie
on the tracks to make a wish come true.

        I made that up.

When I told you everyone stops to kiss
under the arch in Washington Square Park—

        Nobody does that.

I said your eyes are like glaciers and you thought beautiful,
        but what I really meant was cold.

How can I tell you about my eyes? They are so wet,
        they seem invasive to my body.

Kelp brushes my arms and suddenly
        phantom fingers.

I forgot I was suspended in water
        until I wished for its evaporation.

Someone is peering into my emergencies—
        so many blurred colors from above to swallow.

I wish for it to be you but I am nowhere near train tracks,

    so I meditate: *Lincoln, copper, one.*

I still don't understand asking
is the conventional way to get what I want.

All of us are disappearing all the time

When I let in the day, I have to lose a little.
Make space. Disappear. They say humans lose

between 30-40,000 skin cells every hour.
I want to collect them all and make better

versions of myself. Stable skins, cells that stay put.
Live a little. What is permanence if not capturing

everything for keeps? My digital photos and films
will soon disappear too. I don't know what it means

to live in the cloud. The cloud is not real. Outer space
is full of cells and supernovas wishing to explode

in order to disappear. The day is crashing into my cell pile,
scattering what I thought I knew. My fear is that I'll lose

too much at once. More than I can possibly take on
or take back. Texting so much I've shed my fingers

to the quick. Everywhere I touch I leave fingerprints.
On the wine glass at the bar. The table. My iPhone.

Your skin. I bore too many holes into things,
disappearing their corners. Losing myself.

Losing it. I am afraid I'll never regenerate.
The cloud scoops up cells, a sieve for the substance

of myself I'll never get close to touching.
The day never gives back what it stole.

I Was Born a Shrieking Slot Machine

My first word: jackpot. A rolling marquee, one exclamation
point too many. I've only memories of dizzy sevens,
lemons, cherries, and bars. I thought my arms
were handles, levers. I didn't know the players made
the colorful wheels spin, thought my body was called
machine. I'll never know about the Keno Kingdom I inherit,
what conceived the gold in my eyes that everyone said
are like a cascade of coins. He kept me around
because I'm both lucky and volatile. Raised on Miss America
pageants, sizzling filament, taking a chance. The casino
taught me all I need to know about love. Win some,
lose some. If there's jingling, it's littlenecks and oysters
for dinner. But if I can hear the click of the key unlocking
the hotel room's door, it's a quiet ride back. A stop
at a Bob's Big Boy, a piss break and scratch ticket.
Summers let me do whatever: loose bikini tops and salt water
taffy, kissing under the boardwalk and my pickup line, every time
"The only real thing is how fake this all is," how some man
from Tom's River said I needed better reprimand and
a softer shade of lipstick. But I never learn how to
willingly fold. It might sound stupid, but I remember
my father as just the casino, the only version of him I know:
a lead foot down the Garden State, a varying shadow
of fill line on a bucket. And I, the passenger, warming tokens
for the toll plazas between my palms, the hot coins
I toss into the metal basket sparking fires.

My Body Is What Ails Me

Maybe my body hates its skin,
wishes only to be made of water.
Clear, uncongealed, without murk,
film, or blemish. You say,
A summer rash for a summer girl.
But I don't know what that means—
I just want to swim in your pool.
Shock treatment annihilates algae,
so calm until my eyes begin to puff.
I want to sweat chlorine, wish my body
could kill what ails it. Some days
I want to be an ocean but inevitably
I'm more mosquito. Blood corpulent.
Jellyfish sting swollen. Unattractive and pinker.
You ask if I've encountered poison ivy.
It's not weeping. Still we're not touching.
If the world were up to me,
all skin would be resilient.
Fluid never flakes. If it were up to me,
your pool would be all access.
With an outstretched wand,
I'd pick what naturally occurs.
Choose the least inflammatory:
dark monsters that make the bay move,
thick salt, a necessary storm.
The way thunder rolls in and scares nobody.
An ominous purr that beguiles until, soon,
the cellar's wet. Flooded.
I bet my body wants to drown its flesh,
its carrion drifting afloat in the Red Sea.
Writhe and slippery. Suffocated quiet.
O cumbersome body, let flowers bloom
from the hives. Let me cultivate a garden of itch
you'd never want to scratch, a dumb rain
pelting down when the soil gets too dry.

Rock Salt

It can't be salt, just salt, as the reason
the ocean doesn't freeze—a reticent fury
or maybe a thrum in the untouchable underbelly,
its capacity to hold its ships as though
they're tiny replicas in a bottle.
We recall the ocean a certain way,
elusive blue when it's really more dreamscape
grey and its fat froth silhouettes
the skin like it's desperate for a touch,
wants to cup it in its sudden curve. O
when I jump in the Atlantic, I want to be
rock salt, a hollow splash, dissolving into it
dripping nothing but pulse that keeps
vast liquid from freezing, faster
than foxes, fill me full of sharks.
It's blood we say, it can't freeze
because of all this blood inside it—
human, bottom-feeder, whale, cosmic
debris and all the matter and boundless
energy that cannot be created or destroyed.

SPOILED IN SIX WAYS

since you grew up on water   you must not care
ice cream shops   board up   summer quits
king of vacation town   can leave any time
i watch sailboats   from a hill   in New York
can't imagine these houses   their interiors
meticulously groomed   corkscrew stairs
i see a modest blue   house   imagine you small there
with lots of toys   and famous next door neighbors
is Martha Stewart still in jail?   i act like
you're her friend   like there aren't thousands
of streets   that never interrupt each other
like you've touched   the same radishes
and arugula   at the A&P   share Salad Niçoise
recipes   i don't know anyone famous
though once   i thought i saw   James Earl Jones
in a Wal-Mart   if Ginsberg saw Whitman
in a supermarket   i don't think it would be sexy
it would be weird   to see the bounty of our idols
obvious missteps   like preferring marmalade over jam
you & Martha   must make chutneys together
compotes   meringues   i like that you don't care
what people say   this poem calls you spoiled
in six ways and   you still smile at me
when i wear shorts   still smoke pot and speak
French like you were born in Lyon   vacationing there
touching the unshaven hairs   on slender legs
and never learning names   but love the sounds
           of *Nathalie, Hélène, Élise*

All the Flotsam and Jetsam of Hairdo

If you study the pattern, my oceanographer,
then I'll manage the wreckage—
and if the body

is roughly 60% water, I'll allow you
to map these ecosystems within. Demystify
                    all the languid and tumultuous,
what's invisible, surface.
                    Trace the flux.

The mirror is a gyre scribbled into your book:
more hours than notes can hold...
  pompadour, undone. braid.

My hair spun up like a massive
                trash patch in the Pacific
                twisted and taut,

every spritz of Aqua-Net, Bump-it,
                and bobby pin. Lips move *I do it for you,*

            all of it for you—

loose strands are
            beached eels,
a glimmer of electric blue,
                    dried despair.

A one-time plastic tiara with hot glue
                gunned gems, he wrote, *fastened*
                            for disaster

All that the head could expel,
                dark and kelpy. Discarded.

          & Once washed ashore,
          guaranteed back out
          again with next wave.

I think it's time you share
                your method, your research. Tell me now

          how I can hold it
                together.

His Legends Were Like Unicorns

Trying to describe you was psychedelic
like seeing unicorns on Metropolitan Ave.
& Brooklyn was so full of flannel, it flooded
onto the streets. I never trust too much flannel
or facial hair or brown liquids with businessman names.
I arrived on a hunch and you mysteriously manifested
under the laser lights, saturated in artificial blackout.
I used to speak of you in hyperboles, a fiction of royal fabrics.
It's easy to question my veracity but
there must be some truth to every tall tale.
Somehow, I had you in my hand now, not like a text
message but more like a mahjong tile.
Maybe it was some meditative spell, maybe I'm a sorceress.
They say luck is horseshoes and no one knows why
but I know I'd throw them at a stick in the ground all day
if it meant cinching it just once and living to tell.
The night moved only in spaces crushed by colorful beads
shifting in a kaleidoscope, spun in a child's hands.
So then of course a taxi, let someone else navigate the refuge.
Let danger fall peripheral, let's outcharm each other with prowess.
I said, *Take the BQE, it's faster.*
You said, *I'm bringing sleazy back,*
but I don't think sleazy ever went anywhere.
The apartment was like a twitch in a power line
but I let it be candlelit, chandeliered.
I fed you tinctures from my personal collection.
Your blue oxen waited where I left you
sleeping naked on the couch, leather bomber
jacket draped over you— How quickly
we confused mythical and mystical.
How dumb we felt when we realized our error.

No Bulls in the China Cabinet

I don't believe in damaged goods.
When I hear echoing hooves, I change
my locks and shift my space.

A massive monstrosity, a wooden chest
of delicates where all the sparkle lives,
I am pinkies out and parasols so save me
for watercress sandwiches and the like.

27 men in tasseled tops
waving muletas live inside
and you are double the bulls
seeing red in a cabinet full
with neat rows of china.

Think flying cutlery, jaws of life,
the moon's drunk face as cracks
in the windshield spread like liquid.

You know what they say:
Grab the bull by the horns.

You know what they say:
Mess with the bull, get the horns.

You know what I say:
I'm made of matadors and breakables,
swords and sequins, antagonizing reproach.

Pleasure Banquet

Pleasure lives in the land of excess
yes please *more please*, a plentitude.
I want to live where the so-called crisis
does not exist and language is an infrastructure of pleases,
a totality of pleasure. Everything deserves to be touched
if it wants. Everyone is their own fiesta with or without another.
A lover is a man-in-the-moon which is to say a myth
or in outer space. A lover fills a crater
which is to say floats from lack of weight but not empty.
Not empty like there's an abyss elsewhere that we can bridge
with each other but delightfully mundane how the Earth feels
about the moon lackluster in reference but still fascinating,
mystifying. Maybe what we need is an objective source
of all good things because a panic would kill me. So be my moon
my all-you-can-eat buffet yes, even the dentist
is an opportunity for sheer emotional bonding saying *yes*
to everything saying *please* even through gauze.
Let's detonate: remember a totem waxing when the moon
isn't visible it's still there a plastic cup
& when the sky isn't empty it's just longing a phase.

Beard Island, Population: 1

When I woke, your beard said:

This is not a beard

—all mystery unfurled.

Your beard is the fortress surrounding your mouth, the abyss
I must not fall into (if I fall in I'll be doomed),
        an electric blanket with a skeleton of rusty wires,
                a small flitter of spangles
            dusting the sidewalks in a snow globe.

I tease out the tangled thicket
        with canine dentures and damaged sea shells.

It's only as coarse as snow is massive
collected on the ground in quantity.

Your beard's a cocoon for lucid dreams,
        where the television Yule log feels hot
            to the touch and hazy.
The gate of tiny fishhooks where all the hairs curve
        up, parachutes hanging off blimps and clouds.
Your beard's curlicues are springboards in the mattress
        left on the curb, tagged in marker and graffiti—
            flotsam of a college town's moving day.

An island of abundance, miles of scratchy Astroturf,
        a thousand florets I crawl into sometimes,
            lay thin against a follicle,
                hide from uproarious bears.

World-Sized Hole

The sky folds into itself like a clasped hand—
I look up thinking *Does the earth even feel*
comfortable in its own skin? All its textures,
smells, snarl-tooth zippers that never quite clinch.
Elmgrove Ave. has upturned seashells to border
its path: I don't know if they're there to promote growth
or death, what's inside, what water's shore they came from.
Budded bushes behind them always reek of wedding
or funeral. Bountiful bouquets of *Sorry*. I keep flowers
in a spaghetti sauce jar by a window that gets no light.
They shrivel there to suck up that last bit of mending gesture.
I won't move them for days. The flowers don't know the difference,
it's been so long since they've been a seed. Rooted. My skin
has a world-sized hole in it. I'm so tired of writing about it
but I don't know any others. *Just write down your dreams*,
you said. But someone's car alarm is always going off and why
would we ever need cars in dreams? I dream of the world
we know falling apart & this romance is surrounded
by barbed wire. It's the only skin I feel comfortable in.

Spelunker

I need everything mined out of the body
and onto the table. If I were a surgeon,
I'd remove every organ before I could begin
my work, reorganize the cave. Hey mother bear,
is your brethren barren? Do you like the high whine
of winter still winding? I am so not furry but I love
to hibernate. It whets my palate, keeps my coat full.
I don't have any cubs but I'd club you to death
if you get too close. Paws off. I reign supreme
with a floral wreath. I nap under your neighbor's tree
but contrary to popular belief, I'm not a thief. I don't
like honey. It makes me matted. Sticky. But it's true
that I'm clumsy. Good thing I'm not a surgeon.
You'd have to check your guts for rust. For excess.
Or accidental shoelaces where intestines once slept.
Do all animals love shiny things? Are we so predictable
that we get distracted and die? Middle finger in the air crashing
new cars—no one can hear the metal crunch except the trees.

Shatter

when I fall in love   I already know how it will end
a parenthetical like you whisper it knowingly too like
how a memory is punctuated by the weather   when I saw
your face   I imagined you weirder   & when you were
weird   I wondered what I'd done to conjure it   I didn't know
you then   that's impossible   but still I wanted control
o I am so devastated   on the periphery of lives
we'll never live together   my loves never end
in marriage or death   consistently I shatter
into millions of splinters   shards   moondust
mood rings   a spindled story   in the stronghold
of shatter is where I can finally breathe   gimme
some elbow room   a chance to gather   I do not know
why you return if only to help   vacuum the pieces
it sucks   to feel sadness over the end   when it hasn't
even happened yet   it's a simultaneous falling   in and out
like there are dueling pianos   keys clacking faster
& faster   cut the strings   scream cacophony into the streets
my love is waiting for that final push   wait for it
wait for it   latticed bus shelter   cracks and full-length mirrors
we dumpster dive for love   and still wonder why it comes home
battered   why it's faulty and breaking   I need you
broken in a way   where the veins of fracture show   part of love
shattered   is fixing what's broke   a crystalized mass
                                 forming new daggers

The World Is My Rival

I am jealous   of the oranges I picked for you
sliced   like tiny rowboats
there's an impenetrable wall   between inside and outside
The oranges were from me   *Take me with you* they said
into your mouth   citrus fingers   penetrate the wall
I want go through too   covered in blubber
from toe to crown   as if you were
a decomposing sea mammal   I tried to stand on
Too cold to grow in snow   Too many oranges for a carry-on
I cannot go   I am bigger than an orange   I am too big too
jealous of Alaska   I cannot row anywhere
on an orange slice   Is your beard bejeweled
with ice when it rains?   Could we lay supine in the ocean
for a while   just like two glaciers?
Wait   No   I'll become jealous of the ocean
I've lived many lives   you said
a palimpsest I keep trying to claw off every layer
You belong to me as well   the world says
I am jealous   of the states
you live in   the orange slices you share
the words we don't have   the multitudinous parts

Absolutely Cuckoo

I must be crazy   vexed even   besieged by blank avatars
online dating profiles   a cache of cuckoo   holding cards
without faces, numbers, or suits to tip   I built this persona
a curated dilemma   person to toe the tides   but inside I hide
ten thousand tiny tridents   ready to pierce   upward
I'm an anchorless anemone   so run away   and let me go —
I'm vexed   mad with the shivers   bitten by dynamite
what creaks in the night   seeps in the cracks   stumbles out
fumbling for a switch or glass of water   a coronation for corroboration,
I'm crowned queen of crazy liars   like I'd chase you
with a serrated knife   or crash you deep into a fortress
of unmovable beasts. To sleep   with me is to raid
the medicine cabinet—a bad trip   they sometimes say
a hazy fade   Read between the lines   parse the lies
o let me go   xoxo   sudden conjuncture surprises
us in pallid ways.   What I mean   to say is   run
while you can.   The boat   is still docked. Rip down
the curtains   and show us what you've got.   Loneliness
isn't worth brittle backstory   of what's beneath
this mattress of uncomfortable coils   pressing down
and the motley junk shoved underneath   sighing
the cradle   giving up ghosts   between the sheets

"THE LOVER'S DISCOURSE IS TODAY OF AN EXTREME SOLITUDE"

Today is extreme   the solitude   like I am speaking
to you   from one end   of a Chinese finger trap.
The solitude   is the two fingers   trying to meet
and what's said   is caught in the middle
wriggling   woven   and splintering in parts.

Your finger is so close   I can touch it   when I talk
you understand it 67%.   Numbers are relative
or sometimes you say you don't believe in statistics
which means, to me, there's only 0 or 10—
yes or no   and I am not
like that.   Either you get me
or you don't.   Is it even possible to love
the same way?   The difference is what we preserve.
In my dreams   I'm the girl of your dreams

or a woman in sultry get up   in furs.
Is it love   if I don't know what you see
when you look at me from afar   or when
we've spent time apart   and you don't
remember my face   until I've opened the door?
Heavy   the idea of heart hangs   suspended.
What is it that we build with time shared?   A slippery
stone skipping the river.   Murky film   moss & garbage around.
I keep trying to remember   the William Carlos Willams poem
with a flicker of blue   beautiful   in the trash by the train.

Sometimes when what we've built is unraveling,
                              I want you to hold it together.

I conjure the finger trap.   Relax
                and it slides right off. We could live
in the middle of it:
               Woven,
weird, relaxed,

maybe streaked with blue & someone else could find it
beautiful   when an imaginary child chucks it
     in the trash.   I want to tell you that.

Not everything is a metaphor for everything, no deeper meaning
in a finger trap.   Every moment doesn't snowball
       into another   except for when it does.
               I believe in this 100%.

Burden of Desire

> *What*
>   *is desire, if not*
> *this burden. Dearth and glut*
> *cupped in your hands: wild, deadheaded, and blue.*
>   Miguel Murphy, "The Sunlight"

The color of desire is neither
blue nor red, but somewhere
in the middle. Lavender.
Orchid. A mild-mannered
puce, eel streaks of white
electric. A better question
might be what *isn't* desire?
What are the pieces we can-
not hold with our hands?
There's the in-between
of dearth & glut, that middle
where our hands become
a sieve. I began thinking
desire was the sieve but
I'm sure it's what falls through,
what we're always trying
to keep: Pure purple bits
in wild configurations.

Carousel of Iridescence

I want the colors—unstuck, unblurred,
seldom caught one at a time. Here,
behold my collection of rarities:

the tinge of amber
in your barley laugh.
A vial of aquamarine
teardrop. A crack
of coral from a chapped lip.

Dear errant love,
my monocle to capture you best
turned out to be kaleidoscope,
crushes to blood orange pulp.
Onyx. Octopus ink.

The collection is never complete.
You're a carnival of lost treasures,
my plush little nothing, a part to a whole
summer's run—the carneys asleep in the vans
and some wicked switch we flicked
to turn the carousel on.

When did you disappear, you calliope
of dark scales? It's hardly conceivable
that once I knew you. My little droplets
of iridescence I stole are so obscure to me now,
they say nothing of my darts shot into a feeble balloon.

Dear plastic beauty, why won't you
eat sugar from my hand?

Maybe we could have tried something more
pedestrian. A Ferris wheel, perhaps,
with a swinging bucket, metal trap,

no saddles or reins. Dear merciless machine,
I have a strange vertigo and cannot tell
if I am stationary. I am afraid
of the color, of the horses breaking free
from their poles, movement
beyond *up* and *down*.
Dear stupid light, I can't see
the dazzle in your eyes.
Come and get me, stupid light.

Majestic Blues

Sometimes, when I miss you,
colors come spooling out of me
organically. There's no cure
for the majestic blues. O you know
I'm a recluse, some deep longing
ajar like a petulant storm window
haphazardly hung. I am not
weatherproof nor winter ready. If you
never said it, I'd never wear gloves.
Let my hands get so merlot & cracked
in the malevolent January. This feeling
has a majesty, scattered headquarters
manufactured here & solid
as a coveted gem you'd keep
in a velvet drawstring sack. A shot
of Crown for your tribulations. O beautiful
fracture, interrupted amber waves
of grain. How did you fall into my lap?
I was lightly searching. Year of the
Radiant Orchid. Soon the blues
of lesser hues—Halogen. Zephyr.
Illusion. Opal. Wan. I miss you
in a twilight blue. A ball of yarn
unraveling across coasts, loop
and pull. Loose thread in the carpet
systematically undoing
the floor. My heart's carpeted shag,
soft to pass out upon after too many
blue sleeping pills, pulsing
a message: *Don't play fast & loose
with me. Don't sleep here too long.*
Expand your palette & ride
out the whispering blue wind.

The White Diamonds Are a Necklace of Feathers

Whatever it is, you want to contain it,
      grab it by its throat—
make a necklace of white diamonds so iridescent
      it's gaudy.

The hands want what they can't
ever hold, want roots
      where I am forever rootless,
shapes that can't stay true to their forms.
      I might be a run in a nylon stocking,
a sequence of shredding, the underbelly of a snake,
      began of pinhole that expands to expose.

I might run.

I'm like two stones slammed wild. Barefoot
      on hot coals, a malleable fire
always coughing white feathers instead of blood,
      I can't comprehend how *live forever*
      and *never die* are the same.

The surprise never wanes.
      I keep returning to the phoenix,
it's the bird I can't let go.

Parades go by

H.P. Lovecraft   was my neighbor once   I know because
they erected a plaque   commemorating his birth place
I pass it every day   waiting for the parade of buses
while I live here I feel like a vampire   hiding
in the shadows   maybe   I'm dead & don't even know
I love the burning wood & brick oven smell
of the brasserie across from Lovecraft's plaque
& garlic so I'm a horrible vampire   or maybe one
that just won't die   stuck between two hills in the downtown
valley of a wet river   Native American names   abundant
with vowels   harvest to harbor   some of the cops still
ride horses & the horses shit in the streets   parades
go by celebrating smallness   as big as I feel I am also small,
a spectator   waiting to commence.   It's too loud—
trumpets & superfluous car horns   but I love animals
out of context & sequins   balloons & fried foods   gondolas
metal scaled koi. The details pass   the feeling
passes   my therapist says   this is not a forever feeling
*The most merciful thing in the world   is the inability
of the human mind   to correlate all its contents* I am
challenging this mercy every day   I am always forgetting
to be kind   undoing silence is the end of protection:
would you rather be the fanfare   or its sharp & inevitable
end?   In death we are silent   & also protected
the soil is neutral   I am where I am
what I am   is dependent upon it

The City Never Sleeps

despite the city's   impeccably walkable geography
i wish for a chariot   but walk alone   people say
the city never sleeps   they're mostly tourists   the city is
in a coma   i slept on a park bench terribly afraid
of rats   living above Union Square i had a dream
someone mailed me a dead mouse   or maybe just the head
mice used to jump from the oven   roaches in the shower
my life was filthy at best   i walked a lot to avoid
the subway   i loved the thought of having a boyfriend
especially with a car   maintenance of both is incredibly
expensive   i dreamt i ran into you and when I was awake
i ran into you in daydreams   all our haunts are gone
i would trace block lettered handwriting   on posters
follow them like a scavenger map   when i wanted to be anonymous
i'd go to the Olive Garden   a place you'd never be   i traversed
the Williamsburg Bridge from the Lower East Side & felt lucky
despite squandering my time   what if you had said *Let go*   what if
the walk-ups in Chinatown were still cheap   would you live there
with me?   Fill it with art in small frames   potted plants   say forever
to a finite skyline   Can you carry this weight now that we're old?
Remember when you shouldered an easel over the Brooklyn Bridge
you're built strong   i wanted to jump   a body weighs more
or less than that easel   it's no use   eating Popeye's
by the river   wondering why you carried some things & not others
once i watched a girl stick her whole hand & fingers down
a man's throat in Mars Bar   he was puking on himself
& the floor   it was chunky   i spent so much time
on the Lower East Side looking for you   not a tourist
but this isn't home either   so let's build or let go
i don't drive anything   except anyone crazy
but we were connected way before we knew it
like how tourists look for the dirty tile   which i do
every time i'm in Grand Central   because it reminds me of honesty
& simpler times: the city   between moments   catching a nap

When the World Is Trampling Your Safety

Since first I saw you fresh, a wild cluster of moments
have died. Fingertips shushing out a slinky flame.
What freshness wilted around us like wrinkled vegetables
at the farmer's market. When we were young, we were
a whisper. Now we're old and worry. I boom down sidewalks
with such difficulty. I know the way time pillages
what's in proximity. How there's one of two remainders:
wistfulness or regret. A pond to wade in or a fat ocean crashing
the party. Pity peels back a fresh coat of paint. Rusted at the corners,
beckoning the question, *Well, what do we have here?* I'm a too soft
plum plucking grey hairs with a pair of tweezers. You are never
so beautiful as when the world is trampling your safety. It's scary.
Since first the fresh has died, I understand Walt Disney's cryogenically
frozen head. But why wait? When freshness falls asunder, make do.
Post-haste. A grey rain finds a way to dip into the summer day and take
a certain hue away. It regenerates, in its own way. Fresh forges
through new and subtle folds. A rivulet of desire that guides
benign sputterings, which yet, also are green.

Through the Whale

Blood fuchsia and something electric shimmers
in our guts, wings we thought were origami

have real wires, feathers. The underbelly of a whale
is both ridged and bulbous. You say, *This isn't easy,*

because nothing ever is. Because my mood is
moody—so in short, I don't want to hear it.

Maybe later, a letter, with a language I discover
in the water, rubbing against the sand,

the skin of sea creatures in the pit of a faraway
sea. An alphabet untranslatable—I did not know

until now how to transmit this to you.

They say that whales never sleep and neither
does silence, all blubbery and unyielding.

I've slept forever inside this beast, attached myself
to its linings waiting for the right time to surge

outward, bust open the belly. Sounds of trumpet
and screeching, a pewter cloud of ambergris.

In deceptive swirls, hollow Os, the smoke
does all the speaking now and I beseech you:

Let me break open the heavy skin of this whale.

Punk love

hand me down   love   stitched   as though
ripped on purpose   i wanted those fables   for us
tequila on the porch   & astroturf
in the bedroom   maybe I take it too earnestly
I mean all love   is the same   love is a rusted
truck   where a first kiss   once transpired
It's not a best practice   to only say something's
special   when it's gone   like an impossible treasure
out with the trash   I mean it   we were so
young   unwieldy & willing   to lose love
is to give into the idea   that it's already gone

I Think I Spider

Whatever you say, I know it's the thing
you cannot say. Every smile has a hole,
just reach your hand inside and find it.
I love to think of your mouth not as a hole
but a hairline crack. When you say *Baby
I'm a battle ax*, I say *Don't ever let them see you
implode*. Hide your fractures. Your ear is a hole
that doesn't listen. Text me your biggest fear
so I can hold it, feel its weight. If you think of fear
as a pocket-sized rectangle, you can laugh
into its face. I look into you like a luminescent screen.
Our bodies are paradoxically soft and hard, textured
and full of useless holes. When I stop trying
to fill them, they seem to coalesce. I'm a scab-
picker, a puppy newborn with clumsy paws.
Have you met the spider inside of me? It has a shadow,
but it's not just a shadow. I can feel the spider drop to my guts
in one complex parachute. Our bodies are beautiful
webs. An elaborate doily with oblong & futile holes.
The spider says *I wish I was a jellyfish*. I want to ask why
but I know never to ask anything of a wound.

"Wʜᴀᴛ ᴅᴏᴇs ʜᴇᴀʀᴛ ᴍᴇᴀɴ? Tᴏ ʜᴀᴠᴇ ᴄᴏᴜʀᴀɢᴇ. Tᴏ ʟᴏᴠᴇ."

Courage is noble

        but love is forget it. People do

stupid things

        under the influence. I feel a pinch

        in the pit of my chest   like

someone is trying to consume   a whole plum

without piercing   the fruit.   Incisors

    dragging.   What am I ever doing

other than rewriting the story   of myself?

Rewriting and rejecting
        the multitudes.   Instead,

I want to be one
        unmovable thing,

not a phoenix   but like a phoenix   or actually just flame

    defying the science of it.

I want to be held
        like an ocean
                mounts horizon

the heart stammers

                              in protest   against

                                                       the gentle will of
everything

else   stuffed in this body

                                          I imagine

the heart thinks of itself
                              as the only moving part

            but I feel that pull often

like I'm the only person   exploding

in participation   like I want to be completely adorned

                  in gold stars   congratulatory pulsing

In trying to be everything   I forget

                                          the sheer violence of perpetual
movement

                        mallet to xylophone

                              sound

vibrating out   not canary
                                                            but thrashing

the real sounds of the heart
                              we don't know

unless we cup our ears to someone else's

                                    chest

    & try to synchronize

                    let the hearts beat erratic

                  old tickers with
                        subtle voices
                                      know
                                      how the story ends

and the rest   for us

                            is dumb speculation

as we courageously forge on

                            story exploding

                                      behind our spurs

Pity Us Poor Devils

Dazzled by your radiance as though you're more than
boring rock. Smoldering supernova. A shitty lay.
How they swerve into your soft shoulder. Crunched metal
on asphalt. A time to be reckless—unidentifiable after.
I pity poor devils who have no experience
of you and are dazzled by your radiance but once
I was pitiless. A saxicoline creature. Spear-carrier
in my own bed. If you were a keeper, a real catch
among sediment, I was a consolation prize. Unable to survive
in rock alone. *Why do you always look like you've witnessed*
a fatal crash? you asked with my leg slung over your shoulder.
Why couldn't I tell you I hear crawling
beneath the carpet? When you play guitar. Recount
your celebrity in the only three states that know your name.
Make me listen as though I was a red light
to wait through, a traffic jam, a pile-up.
Only the bed could diagnose this myiasis: the sun
broke through the splintered blinds; the sheets;
and heaps of pillows that cocooned you as though
the bed was ready to let out whatever vile and vermin
slept within, like it knew something in that room died.

The Babydaddies

Between the bar and the driveway's crunch underneath your tires—disaster. A sealed fate, phone numbers unrevealed. Nothing left behind. Everybody heard about it in the morning and there's only one thing for certain now: I'm banned from ever seeing the band again.

*

Smoking in the waiting room is prohibited. Maury on the bolted-in TV. *Come*, she said. She said my name. Blown up, swollen—nails clung to sad pink guts. A grainy photograph, she said I could keep it. There's a landscape painting there. I wanted to draw stick figures holding bayonets with Sharpie. No one is looking but it's like everyone is—my guts on surveillance.

*

I called you like I said I would. Your voice reminded me of pimply teens downtown spinning pizza dough in the air, levitation. Last names like Angellucci, Castellano, Lombardi. I don't know your last name. I stop at Nick's and order a meatball sub. I don't even like meatballs.

*

Let's throw a celebration, it's what other people do. All my guests bring gifts in theme— a glass table, an electrical socket, the staircase's plummet that spirals and thuds. I said *Bring me a gift I won't want to take back*. Bring me a gift. Deliver it.

*

She used the word *shedding*, said a great deal of debris is inside my body, a thriving city blown apart by an atomic bomb. I wanted to tell you about tossing stones, that's how it feels. How they skate across the film of the Hudson before they sink with relief, that you are the only souvenir left from the wreckage. That last stone, past skating, sinking into the river's abyss.

*

Last night, I heard, you totaled your car after the bar. These are the parents we could have been: a cherubic infant face smothered by an air bag that only deflates too late. A face with no fruition, sticky with strawberry preserves and cereal crumbs. *How could you bring a baby to a bar?* but these are the actual parents. A family in the front seat on purpose, snuffed out the same way it arrived. And this conspiracy is the only magic between two people: A portrait of who we are, deepest shades of inherent killer—all I'll ever know.

You don't have to wear the red hat

I watch shoppers graze produce   inspired
by their attention to selection   their slow-
down   everything moves too fast these days
panic but no urgency   I bet someone does
your shopping for you   there's no satisfaction
in the arena of strewn capital   I don't believe
in societal curtsy   and cotillion
a husband was an item   box to check

tidying your name   turning down your gloves
to the homeless   when this is more their home
than yours   the trains politely ask you
      to leave but   you persist in pleats & platitudes

where i'm from   my tea isn't sweet

                              nothing is
     in fact the sweetest thing   is everything recklessly
without approval   or mythology
my family crest is escape   yours owns a plantation

O I don't want to be polite
         or know how   to delicately say anything

my selection is slow   my life is unmarried
and nameable   that's the problem you see
where i'm from doesn't name   the buried
if *where I align* were your mantra

O no more sharp lines of success
    items to cross off   realness makes me
complete   feel completed   completely in control
       no offense   but the husband quest
is desperate   disturbing   your ring teeters
on tacky   I say it like I would to a friend

when you've nothing to hide

spare me nothing except what's real   no pretense
of an outward niceness   cursing up a storm
like it's cute to be common   O I don't say this often
but why pretend you don't want it there   love it even
where America believes   it can be great again
you don't have to
wear the red hat   for me to know
                what your heart is made of

"YOU LEAVE THE ROOM ALL AT ONCE"
after akp

No one ever leaves a room all at once. No one
has the weight of their departure pinned so tacitly.
When you leave, the air around you is strewn about,
ajar, like it was tough to cut and now gaping, gasping
for its severed chunk. When we say passing time,
when we say filling the gaps. It's the room that needs
it. Something to do with all this hot air, all the
fragments that just won't leave. There's a certain
violence I tether to leaving, bursting through
a smooth surface. Disheveling what's soft & light.
A gathering of what's left behind to ship back
to you, no note inside. It's so dramatic, the leaving,
the return: Collect what forgot to come with you
and clear the air of what you didn't mean to leave.

The Soft Center of the Earth

When the world was flat, we were so afraid
we'd fall off the edge. I never left the town
lines but now I want to be the first
to touch the earth's hidden center.
I want to know if it's hot to touch— is there lava?
Will my hand melt, bone and all, into a puddle
of charred marrow? Is a scream trapped
in the pit? A landfill of dreams or a nest
for quiet pigeons? Will it bleed? Are you afraid
to get too close, to drown in its oil spill?
Come on—I want to know what you're afraid of.
I'll climb a ladder made of tree branch and shake
the stars out of the sky. Wield them like weapons
to puncture this shell. Pull out the guts of this world,
all its innards, like pink party streamers in the wind.
Look out your window, what do you see?
No lines or curvature, just endless pulsing
water. Maybe the explorers chose a circle,
trailed its massive backside as evidence
and like it best that way. What if
our planet is actually nothing
but a hollow? A global wound.
Natural and devious. A mass dislodged,
forlorn in space. Gasoline rainbow.

Free to be without

I am rubbing against the day   with all
the answers   they are malleable   malevolent
slippery sometimes   when I am sleeping
I am most myself   peace signs up   I am perpetually
out   I'm like so far gone before I arrive   first
to roll up my yoga mat   there is nothing   there is
nothing   there is emptiness and comfort in that
but I am never comfortable   in fact   I suspect
I sleep with too many pillows   my sweater
is itchy   nothing matters except that
we're warm and well-fed   or laughter
above all   or free to be   alive or alone
the silence finds me   like a scream
when you're scared and I can't have
all the answers   they change   if they don't
they're not the answers   what am I searching
for?   questions   the end of the question—
Wheres reaching for *Whys   Whoms* saying *unplug
lose control   disconnect and disengage
take care   stand up   you have the right to
remain silent*   comfort in its own right is alive
I am churning with answers   that afford
more questions   questions are king   I ask
therefore I'm alive   therefore I can sleep
stowed away in dreams   free to be without
boundaries or boldness   it is so quiet in here now
when you're alone you can assess the carnage
of yourself   cup silence in your hand like
a small child's cheek   as he looks to you
for something   assess tenderly   there's nothing
to do   tendencies have nowhere to be
it's the only answer I need   a question splitting
and dividing into more   asking in silence
circling   an unnamable perimeter

THAT MAKES YOU SO EASY NOBODY AFTER

Maybe time moves too fast—it's all sausage to me. But
I'm just here to sing a song about psychedelics & see
how the sausage is made. Can you help me? It's so easy—
The sausage was a baby. Now the baby lives in different casing.
Once you've had one, there's nobody after, even if more come.
My poor little sausage, my mincemeat pie. I don't believe
I minced my words: it's easier once you're gone. Once I know
where I'm going to go. First, the bundle squalors out,
then it's stripped away. When I was born, I was so jaundiced
and shriveled. Imagine only yellow forever. Think melting butter
over mashed potatoes. A slimy film. Cholesterol. A man
showed me a picture of a dead baby outside of Planned Parenthood.
He yelled *Ask them to show you your sonogram* but I walked in there
so barren. The opposite of pregnant. Instead of becoming fuller,
I only recede and implode. Get emptier. I am nobody after
I am somebody, I lose a piece of me each day. In the bathroom,
there are directions on how to wash your hands. *Wash your hands
of this* they say, which doesn't even make any sense. Scrub and still
there's hands. Hands doing no good, making messes. Take it easy.
No one takes it easy better than you. The chillest. Truthfully, I am
googling translations of German idioms because I am not smart
enough to decipher what this means. I'm nobody's sausage
nor pig in a blanket. It's so easy to love you. There's nobody after.
Some women eat the placenta. When I put you in, there's no way to stop
you from leaving. I am learning how to wash my hands. There's nobody
after you. It's easier alone. I can't think of an interpretation as sad.

Selfie at 29

Nothing is ever plain,
    not even this excessive snow
        lazing about
too early to contain
    a glint of glittered night and I am
fucked in that   I still don't know how to shrink.
I still think our love was like a geode
        rock and I know that's dumb
to say out loud, like you should
        go around smashing everything
    to see if what's inside is beautiful.

Go ahead and smash this, unearth
    all these bedazzled fragments
  if they even still exist. Instead,
    remember me some other age,
      your witchy ethereal.

The city clamors with me. I've got
    big cement shoes to fill.

What I love most about the geode
    is that it's hollow.
  So is this affirmation:
    Home is a hollow rock,
    I fill the space within.
    Live off what little light
      it gives.

Your love gave off little light. I wanted
  to smash it often. Listen,
    I woke up with a knife
      in my hand. A rock
  is not a bandage. I don't know why
    anyone would treat it like one.

        Listen, simplicity is
inherently complicated. A rock
never dreams of being anything
            other than a rock but
        a broken jar can become beach glass.

Instead of stealing the beach glass
        you found in Narragansett I wish
        we buried it. I wish we found
a way to split this geode evenly,
        nestle the beach glass inside
seal the edges shut. A slice so clean
        its scars a smooth pattern.

Every geode conceals
        a secret. The only way
        to keep anything
            simple
                is to never find it.

The Triangle

My rivalrous desire is triangular, a litmus test
for lovers. Is it so wrong to hold onto throbbing
stings if they're the only crutch you have?
What's the alternative? I google her name
over and over and still don't know what I'm searching for.
I won't touch the broken mirrors you carry in your pockets.
Is that a heap of fractured glass in your pants or are you
always this austere? Don't deny me my affect,
my dallied dynamic. We're so obsessed with the wild
vines flashing ornamental berries across the wall
we forgot about the rot. There's no eternal summer
vaulted in this spoiled body. Everyone loves a good origin
story and I've spent this steel wool time unfolding
the origami of my unfortunate pleats, scorning
all fingers that made us into cranes likely never
taking flight. My flippant love is a frayed wire,
which is better than your duplicitous broken mirrors.
Last night I dreamt I collapsed in a field of wheat,
suffocated in gentle piles. The bed I slept in filled
with silverfish. I am a woman who cannot be saved
or rather I dream of regeneration constantly—the mirror,
magnification and the magic. I asked her in the dream
if wheat was flammable and we danced barefoot
on our carnage. My affect oscillates. I asked her
where she's from and she pointed at you and when
she asked me where I'm from, I pointed at the vine
on the wall. Look hard enough at anything
and you'll find what you desire.

Chill

The weather lady said *Arctic chill*
but I woke up sweating, woke up
to the crass cymbals of clanging pipes
& swelling ceiling fissures. Hiss soundly,
hiss quiet if it means you'll soon shut up
for real. My text messages are so full
of bombast and emojis. Numbers
have the ability to scare me. I see 26
unread messages and I want to tell
my immediate contacts: *Cool it.*
I want to coin the next big thing for *cool
it*: ice off, freeze in a pond, not if you had
the biggest icicles. Might send a text
to V with a knife, confetti, a skull,
& praying hands. How do I indicate heat
as a tangible item? I want you to know
it's hot, for one, and disruptive, incredibly
boisterous. If all your current girlfriends
could text me a raised hands emoji,
that would be great. Let's go inside the pipes,
let's shut up. Let us be the last heatwave on earth.
I don't need to calm down, to cool it. I'm vexed
at the cold but I'm obsessed with my pipes
how they kept me up for 48 hrs. straight
and everything looked like a Barbie's
face nuked in the microwave, a plastic
topographic disaster. Don't sweat, let me
see those hands. In one hand's a gun
& the other a pill. Choose one and make it
wisely. Don't follow me through the pipes
if you know what's good for you. I'm looking
out for me. There's steam right before the sound
and a quake right before a periodic silence.
Things are heating up here now—
don't tell me to chill.

Hexes & Curses

The curse begins with your name
but I don't know it so I can't say it.
So I begin with what I know. I curse the state
where you live and say its syllables in staccato:
Flor-i-da. I make the last syllable sound
vitriolic in my mouth, *duh*, like stupid,
like spitting up penicillin taste. I curse
any memory with you in it, whatever you did,
it's cursed now. If you have an accent,
I curse it. If you don't, I curse it too.
May your Macbook be cursed, the one you use
to write your emails, and may you blame
its malfunctions on Mercury Retrograde,
even when you purchase a replacement
and it malfunctions too. Your emails
so insignificant, even the mailer daemon
doesn't deliver them back. The thought of them
electrifies your home, sparks shoot out the outlets,
shocks your family members and pets. I curse
the key holes in your home so they're slightly askew,
and unlocking the door's a struggle. Look,
I mean no harm but if someone in the shadows
followed you down your dark driveway, I curse you
to choose correctly—slice out his eyes with the keys
or struggle to unlock the door and hide inside. Let me tell you
a secret though, the door is cursed. I curse it to be easy to kick down.
So when I drive down to confront you, I am the wolf,
you're the little pig. Your house is made of straw. This curse
sets it aflame. Your garden is burning and the whole block smells
of toasted marshmallow and freesia. I don't know if they have freesia
in Florida so I'm cursing you with invasive plants that strangle the life
out of your wanted ones. I didn't want this incantation. Until you
wrote to him, I had no need for curses or hexes. I did not know
where Florida was other than South of here, over the way,
I did not know he knew people in Florida, that he slept

on your couch or maybe in your arms. I curse your arms.
May they turn to rubber as you carry in glass bottles of gin
and lemonade for cocktails. May the paper sacks break and birds peck
at your bread bags and when you visit the pond in your backyard
for solace, I curse your reflection to only reveal what you look like
in death. I suspect you put a curse on me. I suspect you tamper with
my keys. I curse you to be pretty and kind and bound in protection
from harm, to cancel out the curse you've put on me.

Obsessed with the Emails

the emails are intrusive   ruined everything
cyber space is not alternative space   in a human
I'm a human not an inbox   not an avatar
hey what's your email address   *first name dot*
last name at boring domain dot net   the sound
of dial-up gives me comfort when nothing else
can which is fucked up   if you know what
happened   O static   O remixed digits in the night
O short-hand poetry online   Love is my favorite
technology   God of destruction   digital meltdown
Obsession with the emails   defined
in a moment of history   divulged
to a private party   kicking the machine
I want to be a hero   it's not a crime
to email your friends   but might as well be
to be bad   indulge in cheesecake   I have no sense
of humor   this is not a political poem
the personal is insular   involuntary   where emotion
goes to die   would you love me if I cried more
or less?   I am using love to gauge my self-worth
want all your words   but you're secured   password
protected   and I can't sleep   locked out   guessing
the combinations   without trying
the obvious: her name   beneath asterisks

Homewrecking is a Chain Letter

Homewrecking is a chain letter,
pass it on. I mean, what a weird phrase,
like it takes two to make a home. I live
in a museum of tacky figurines, Ikea end tables.
I didn't need a third to wreck my own yet here I am
setting fire to the Internet. When I sleep,
I accidentally enter your dreams
to watch you love other women. I get the same
letter over and over, never have my moment.
I don't know who wrote it initially but it's
probably in the Bible taking on certain mythologies.
Some stories are so ingrained. So cliché. I yawn
every day because I've heard this one before.
When someone tells you it's nothing,
they're lying. Listen, you don't know
what I'm capable of. I built this island
before I read the Odyssey. Man-made
monsters cloistered in my closet, sequestered.
No one is kind to Calypso or understands
the archive of e-mails she must've had to read.
Any woman outside of love would pull the modem
plug, but I let you plug along. How many e-mails
written next to me? How many e-mails in the bed?
Being a woman in love feels sometimes like
a chain letter. Forwarded along to the next.
O I am so empty when I think about the abundance
of words that can't be placed. The ones that find
their way in unlikely folders. My borrowed time,
my tired narrative. Give me a lover who's never
had another or relief from the loop of liars. Let me
sleep and not seep into unwanted dreams, stop
reading into it, seeing something damning where
there was only something sweet. Could someone
explain if it's the wrecking or the home that
causes the initial problem? How about we say
nothing forever and let the silence speak on.

Consider the Obvious

no one human is the center. The center is hot
and intergalactic. My center however is human.

It's the only scaffolding I have. I say *Center*
over and over in the mirror.

Center is my totem word. The mirror is
where I look when I am lost, when I forget

what I am and what I've taken. Everyone is
taking, discarding a little and keeping morsels

of energy. Keeping tabs. Keepsakes.
I don't believe in cherishing a box of objects,

whether minor or precious. For you,
I have so many questions. How many beds

are in your residence? On a scale of 1-10,
how would you evaluate your correspondence skills?

Are you smart? Do you keep a box of trinkets
under the bed? Depending on your answer

to the first question, which one?

I am writing you a letter without reading yours.
When you intend a recipient, there are no guarantees.

Your words aren't for me, but its contents
are open. I'm a constant recipient of addresses

I never wish to know. Narratives that don't need me
to carry the voices, yet here I am, a vessel

of history. I fall and weave—my center
is a loom. Every letter is born out of purpose.

What do you need to say? Why
do you have dominion over the center?

What, if anything, are you holding onto?
And what will it take to get you to let it go?

The Unnamed War

Did you leave a nightlight on? Turn down
the sheets? Did you fix coffee in the morning
from a french press? Do you know the way
he likes the pillows thin and flat? Did you
shower together, all soap & morning detritus,
or give the illusion of separate beds? Did you
enjoy a modest breakfast together on the porch
of poached eggs & fresh grapes from the vines?
Did you know that I imagined this so I'm in it
now? I'm surveillance. The question you must
answer, the lenses in the walls. My microphone
picks up everything. Some say it's a curse
to be this observant, but the bigger curse is to
live inside a wall. To know one fact and breed
an infestation of questions. Is your hair brown?
Does it dam up the drain in the tub? Does he
gingerly pluck it out and stick it to the tile?
Does this aggravate you? Do you know the way
it irritates me? Are you pretty? I mean, does he
call you pretty? Do you drink wine at dinner?
Whiskey after dinner? Are you over this
interrogation? I'm over it. I live in a shadow,
inside all the shadows. You are the sunshine
and I am the shadow. I am nothing like you,
nothing new. I wish I was a clone instead
of a free agent. Isn't that strange? I'd rather
know the cues than invent my own? To be
alive is a burden, a lonely exploration
of an uninhabitable woods. Do you live in
the woods? Do you have a porch swing?
A net for catching mosquitos? Or a jar
full of fireflies? Are you so enamored
with warm weather? The South? Do you
think it's not even sticky? I know you must
have perfect hair that's neither flat nor frizzy.

I know the wars you've already won. I should surrender. But the truth is that this never stops. The war is never over. You only know me by description but we are fighting all the time.

Bones of our assembly

The world is so small
it would eat itself if it could.

A curtain changes morning's color,
a face fractured in sluiced light.

Whatever the heart wants
it wrenches, whatever else
it wretches. Death is within me,
dormant for now. I don't want to be

friend-zoned by death. My body is a temple,
the temple of *No Thanks*. Bone buttresses its tent
as though shelter is a viable option here. My body
speaks the inexorable language of *Whatever*.

You always say *My God*
like it's yours alone.
My God in amazement, *My God*
in exasperation, *My God* of humility
and grace. Who doesn't have God
on speed dial? PCP never solved any problems
except *How do I get more bloody?*

My body is a shelter of runaway feelings.
If it had an account, I'd *What's Up* Death
on Twitter. A three-way phone call,
God, Death, and me.

Why do we put flowers on graves
when those, too, die? The world, at scale,
could fit in Death's pocket. No one
ever says, *My spirit animal is human.*

Which is colder: this bathroom floor
or space? My bones are little
mandarin oranges in a Jell-o mold.
I want to trademark the way
your jaw clicks when you chew on them.

God is the opposite of death,
but death is not the opposite of life.

My bones left flowers
for your bones,
but they've all blown away.

It's more like pallor,
not a fissure,
and heartbroken
is an inaccurate term.

Death is alive in every love. Hey,
here's a more accurate term:
dead libido.

Do not Namaste me,
my soul has left the building.

Divide is more accurate
than divine. My body slept
through entire years, missing
birthday parties for its bones.

Bow to my celestial ennui,
a salutation to the stagnant.

For you, I wish to be a turn-
key, but let's keep it real:
I'm actually a fixer-upper.

Catching Up Is a Form of Keeping On

When you write a letter, you are forcing yourself
inside thought. Triggering a synapse, a sequence.
Memory is a many tethered thing, a man in the moon.
Looking upward, I see. Remember? Maybe it was
a moment shared. Or a clean-shaven man's cologne
on the subway. A similar shoe. Maybe there's no logic
to it. It arrived and, suddenly, an outpouring. An outlet.
I don't believe in coincidence or rather nothing
is incidental. Catching up is a form of keeping on,
persisting. Holding close. Inserting yourself. Love is
my trigger word. When there is love all around, there's trouble.
A jagged edge splits fear of the past and love for the future,
or maybe its inverse. What I'm trying to say is you loved once,
and it's over, but if we talk about it, then there's trouble.
Things get sticky. Stuck. Stuttering on why, when
you close a loop, you'd then try to pry it open.

The Skittering Centipedes

What I love about the skittering centipedes in my apartment is how they move across the carpet in camouflage. Eye trick. Too quick to adjust, the moment you realize, they're gone. I'd love to be invisible like that. Leave only the trace. When you're wistful, you want to share, but it's best if there's no commitment. I wonder if you expected no response, if your intent is truly benign. I could write about this for hours. Your ability to move mountains consumes me. Geographically we're not close but I feel you breathing down my neck. Every past lover is a wolf in a cashmere sweater. Yesterday's rabbit. Something so soft with canine teeth. Maybe you didn't mean to but it's slashing me asunder, like beneath your sweater is a locket and only the three of us know what's inside. I'm in on a secret that's shattered me. And you know what they say: What's gone is gone. What's good is also gone. When the good gets going. When the going is gone. Say your salutations and sayonaras in the same beat. Because your mouth couldn't handle both, we're all still saying. Well, you're still saying. I'm the invisible bystander, the whoms it may concern you might not have stopped to consider. Damage trickles down, a long body with little legs. Think of yourself setting it in motion. Think of yourself as the top of the chain.

No chill is my given name

My anxiety precedes the internet age   I worry
about everything   even as a kid   always
worrying   the internet exacerbates   power
is knowledge but this rootless knowledge leaves me
powerless   I shouldn't be allowed to find your exes
see on Google Earth   houses you shared
before a dog with a bone there was someone like me
obsessed with search engines   dogs are not like me
I'm not man's best friend   if you haven't guessed
I have zero chill   no chill is my given name
millennial phrases make me feel semi-chill   like
I am all about that hustle before hustle was a thing
because if I don't keep moving   my anxiety will literally
swallow me   if I stop I won't stop at all   I'm not chill
I feel shame about everything   fear of the Ouija board
and oversharing   needing more napkins at lunch
period chatter & bloated   I know I'm my best enemy
because I'm fixated   frothing with intensity   I will
beat myself up and blog about it   searchable sadness
simmering in a machine   kindness lives in chill
but I am not permitted to enter   call it high strung
wound tight   the chorus of everyone whispering
       you're not
              supposed to talk about it
I'm mummified in sheaths of staleness   sayings I don't want
to take with me to the sarcophagus   *stop it!*
excessive nagging   not sand or slippery
quite strong actually   if I knew how to stop
I would   all these voices   confuse me
the internet is an archive   frivolous fingers   words
to keep for ourselves if we knew anything good
for us   googling remedies   googling forgiveness
googling how to love   when you have no chill
when you're obsessed with the e-mails   writing forever
without resolution   someday these words

will mean nothing   my anxiety will shrivel up
with me   the internet is the only forever I'll know

There Goes the Neighborhood

I could lay our selfies side by side   lie in mud and   drag it
through the house   she dismantled.   When I think
about the men   where I lie   I feel occasional, a ghost.
I tend   to their dismantled houses,   built with parts
from borrowed foundations. The lives lived, transient
through the weaving.   What are the pure parts
of envy?   I want her to like me even though
she doesn't know me.   Is that too passive or
aggressive to want everyone to want to be your best
friend without obligation   or consequence?   I think
she's horrible,   duck-lipped and maybe
with dogs.   When a lover takes another lover,
there's an imprint.   The mattress is confused. I envy
the terraces and hanging baskets of petunia, rhododendron.
I'm a perpetual renter.   The love I have is leased
by an owner who won't sell.   Good riddance
to the wind and   o god all these locusts centipedes crock
pots and cross-eyed promises. I wanted a pretty house
to share.   Her wooden rings from mugs on the counter
keep me up at night. A loose connection, a loss, a commentary
on where   the neighborhood went.   I envy a history
empty. I see why the downstaters eradicate the trees
and build tremendous houses plain & untouched   bloated
with appliances, no memories to encounter. A bounty of rooms
that have never been muddied   no ghosts to bump into inside.

Homewrecking is Different from Housebroken

Homewrecking is different from house-
broken, in fact, some might say
they're opposites. When I think of myself
I think you have picked the lock,
sat naked comfortably on a leathery
surface. I don't break the windows anymore;
I got smart. I'm a good girl. I know
you can see through them. *Window*
means *glass*, means *now I can see*, or
crystal clear, as one might say. Take me
terribly tinted. Stained glass. Do your
other women know about me, about the
windows I am & see through? Peeping Tom
leering into your public space o god all I want
is to trust that where I lie is truth. I see
a guardrail and know I must accelerate,
ignite. Burn this whole place down.
Whenever we are driving somewhere, I think
I wish I was home, but it's broken. Wrecked.
I put fresh water in the vases every day and
what good did that do? It's not something
a set of tools from your grandfather could fix.
It's clear to me now, that the home is an extension
of yourself. If it's tidy, there's no problem.
The windows are open; you can see inside.
O can't you see that nothing is what it seems.
We have curtains & draw them billowing
extravagance to say we're still here
but cloaked. Hidden. Unable to interact
with the unwelcome & unbearably bright light.

SAY GOODNIGHT

Why you would take the time when you don't
even say goodnight anymore
      don't even wear the cologne or go out
of your way   what about good morning
   a check on my well-being   I am a hissing crock pot
a creaking door to fine-tune   someone you most definitely
   hide from in the garage   pretend to enjoy engines
& drills   writing is my shut up time   yours is for catching up
with old flames   which I like as the word for her
since it sounds like a forest fire   like it's been perpetual,
burning in the periphery   you said you hate writing
you like it now   you said she is amazing
I've never heard you say that about me
   on paper I sound pretty good   until I remember
pretty good's got nothing on history   when I was young
I did regrettable things   I mean if you didn't you were born old
or yesterday   some old saying   I don't know what it's like
     to want to be a mother   many women tell me I must not
be a real woman   sometimes I wish I wasn't
sometimes being a woman feels like   filing your taxes
every day   without an accountant   I'm a registry of stupid
   expenses   a greasy pile of unreadable receipts
you keep a ledger of my worth somewhere   under the mattress
   when you included her in amazing   you excluded
all else   I'm amazed by nothing   everything amazing is not
   mine to experience   I watch sunsets alone
draw the curtains dramatically   kiss myself goodnight

With Change Machine and Pearls

If she wants to wear the flapper dress and pearls
to the laundromat, let her wear the flapper dress and pearls.

Let her bend and toss towels, brassieres,
and garments to the *shhh shhh* of her nylons.

Don't blame her bejeweled frock on laundry day,
everyone who gets dressed in the morning

dresses up in drag. The quarter machine spits back bills
like blown raspberries. Everyone looks—

are the colors bright? Lace or cotton and what else
into the bottomless metal cube oscillating

her dirt, her soapy brine? Blouses puffing up
like plastic bags, the *shhh shhh* against tree trunks.

She watches you, watching, back and forth. Clean clothes
take a while, must wait for them to wash, to dry.

The basket's a sad coop for lost socks, jaundiced walls
the shade of chicken grease, an archipelago of stain.

String of pearls wrap around her throat, grind together
when she pulls on the loose loops. The big sequins

mesmerize. Children stare, *is it her birthday?* They think
she's out of a stuffed mirrorball, black confetti.

Uncloaked, she's all flesh and innocuous, *sorry
to report*, kind of flippantly she says. Unapologetic.

There are cleansing properties in just water—no use
wondering if the laundry will ever get clean,

if she'll ever remember to air dry the bras, to change the temperature settings, check the pockets.

A pearl in a scalloped clam, some wave that never crashes. Move through the day like a riptide.

The cactus where a heart should be

What died and grew   in its place   prickly pear
   or is there underneath   a sea anemone
protecting its core   & all around barbed wire
vipers   razorblades   a moat of alligators
hippopotamuses that could obliterate   crunch
the skulls of any trespassers   the heart is a stand-in
for what   is a stand in for courtesy   affection
for moxie   spark   modern romance   a stand in
for the ways we do   & don't   hurt each other
what we're capable of   the inability to articulate
what any of that means so my heart   is a saguaro
leaks & bleeds   irregular   looks like tropical fruits
& desert ornaments   these walls build themselves
or rather,   first slurp   then develop the sturdy
epidermis   of course, at first   there's breath
then the retention of water   tell its fortune
in tea leaves   read & keep them   until they rot

Horses Can't Swim

Drowning in hurricanes
               the neighing swept under wind
                    wails like a secret.

I don't remember
               if there was a song
                    trilling of bolt
                    & screw.

I longed for human touch
               on my wooden skin
                    but just water.

               Wave fingers. Gust fist.

Horses can't swim
               so I said a prayer
               and the prayer spoke back:
               Wood is buoyant.

We can't float beneath iron rods,
               the city's
                    scattered skeleton.

Nature always tries to pull big,
               wreck your cluster.
               But isn't that what makes the carousel
                    spin? The marrow in my tilt?

I wanted you then—whole,
               here, dry. I wanted you
                    as a raft of rabbit fur
             with many strands to cling to.

I wanted to be a mouse
        swilling from a thimble. I wanted that
        for all of us. A liberated carriage,
                the strength to turn this drowning box
                      into a rickshaw, an escape. A boat.

Bright Red Bit

When our beta died, we dumped him
bowl and all into the Susquehanna. O
I was so sad without a fish. The dark bellowing
ring in the wood where the bowl once was.
Why didn't we save even one marble?
As I sprinkled his food into the river Jeff said
You killed it, and I knew he didn't mean the fish.
Sometimes I'd walk down Hawley if only
to see if a bowl was floating in the glints
of diurnal water. I like to think our fish is
the river now and I swear I saw a bright red bit
at the bottom, unlike how we found him
cadaver grey. When I die, I do not really want
my possessions with me down there, returned to earth.
Just stuff I pulverized into a nurturing. My home,
for one, as rotten as it was. The red Solo cups
on the porch, the second-hand bed, dirty
tube socks and loose threads of tobacco in the carpet.
I left before the flood, but I hoped our fish
would come back, a message in a bottle
uncorked. The message might've said: *Always
be an endless stream of regeneration,*
which was sad since that was impossible
for us. We were more like the glass bowl, might've been
screaming until it broke. I was always underwater
with our fish swimming through the little crevices of
the plastic castle and the rainbow flakes of food,
the debris in the river and the cardboard boxes full
of things I could never take with me when I die.
If I could give you a message from the Susquehanna,
it would say that there's a limit to perseverance.
How our fish must've known his sighs were numbered
when I noticed his tattered fins as fragile and broken harps,
while unhooking frames from the wall, packing boxes.
That fish was what I loved about the Southern Tier

and there is nothing like the love for something
that will never love you back.

JE ME SOUVIENS

Driving along   *je me souviens*   the license plate says
I remember or rather   I myself come again   on a whim
it would be an understatement to call this an obstacle   in my path
or road block   leading to detour   more like our paths loop
and if you're not careful   its looping gains infinity   a vehicle
road made for horses of past times   remembered   in no real
specificity   just that I know there were once horses   clomping
hooves instead of cars   carelessly blowing through lights
this is the part where I tell you what I remember   except I think
you know more than I do   I wish I had my own historian
or could write   a biography on the slippage of time   my four years
living as a shadow   compartmentalizing desire   misplacing
the meaning   needing   what people seek in religion
we govern ourselves   when we ask someone else
to take the wheel   like I don't even have a driver's license
I'm genuinely scared of my inattentiveness   my tendency to
let go   when the reins need more pulling than ever
I don't remember   how I got this way   and I don't let therapists
write that narrative for me   although they try   to orchestrate
car wreck   on the edge of losing something you can't regenerate
dip your toes   in the thick spill of it   or never remember
almost losing   O I remember now
I'm a natural disaster   in reaction to the atmospheres around

From a Supermarket

The supermarket of my desire   flush with citrus
perfectly aligned boxes & labels   as seen on TV
in a dream   my brother was counting apples
locally sourced from a nearby farm   it was New York
City   dim-lit and dirty   he made a friend
in fingerless gloves   your whole family was there
and I wanted you   but my brother was lost
escalators so narrow   there is no currency   no tender
when I am sleeping I'm more nervous   than when
I am awake   this may seem like exaggeration
but everything in relation to me   is far away
when I lived there   I shopped in bodegas
pet their cats   ate egg sandwiches on Kaiser rolls
for so many people   this place is lonely
in my dreams it's a danger zone   I wonder why
ever again you leave me   thin-sliced
where there's everything you've ever wanted
you need more   you need me in better quality
or quantity   when it's lacking you linger elsewhere
there's a Whole Foods on Union Square now   I don't
know if the Food Emporium is still there   but
in a dream I am every supermarket   large
and tidy   abundant with space   hexagonal display
delivered from forever   fresh baked bread
breathless symmetry   when I wake up I cry
then write from a Price Chopper   in suburbia
were you happier than you'd ever been   how
does the subconscious have its finger on an unspoken
pulse   shopping feels good   to actualize a loss
hemorrhaging money   when the body can't

Accuracy & Precision

No love is original
  & there's no replica
    for experience.
Photos are not translatable
    artifacts. No one knows why
we never love the same
  or why the false mustaches we bought
only stuck for a few hours.
    We wore them
      to the supermarket, frolicking
between Pringles cans and fresh baked rolls,
    hanging halal goats in the case.
A stocker yelled,
    "Those dudes are girls!" and how
    our laughter interrupted
      the air with *duh*.
We love people without explanation. Kind of
  like religion—we believe without question,
or at least, if we're doing it right.

Best friends boast different love
    than boyfriends or brothers.
There's no nuance
  to the language even though
    it's done in different ways.
I love freaking out
  the baggers at the market
and I framed the photo
  in my house as an altar
    to the way whimsy wields us.
How love isn't controlled
    or contained. My friend and I
      discuss Roland Barthes and wonder
what we'd even do if we had a language
  that could accurately express.

My boyfriend tells me
        there's a distinct difference
                between accuracy
                      and precision.
I watch his little breaths as he sleeps.
        His mustache is real.
I ask him if he loves me, and
        he says of course.
I wonder if this assessment is
        accurate or precise.

What keeps me from believing,
        when we believe in the language of others,
                especially the doubting?

The weather inside me is raining.
        All the time. It's the only thing that stays.
        Love
            is unoriginal
        when it's me and I'm making it.
I said it before. I know
        the end
& the fragments
        that make it so   unbearably leaden.

Elegy

The reporters said there was blood
on her legs. We said, *oh no, she wouldn't*

damage those—we remembered her poise,
accentuated muscle, how they called her

The Voice, but we called her The Legs,
remembered it better than the bad interviews,

where she said *Crack is whack*, when we said
So sad, when we blamed it on Bobby.

I focused on the clock, sobbing
out the time, stricken hours, the TV's

crackle and all its horrible humidity.
My breakdown was not broadcast

but I, too, was on the floor with nobody
who loved me. All I had were capsule shells

like cast-off claws from a baby monster.
A culmination of things once killed me.

When we were living, I called you *Monster*.
When we were dead, I called you *Bobby*.

Say you wanna dance I said, but we
were only shells. Nothing of substance.

We heard the news say *accident*, felt sad
but we liked that word, used it for our own.

I needed a bath to be just a bath, just
to loosen crimped and lacquered hair,

all my days belabored into restless nights.
I needed to loosen the grip of your claws

fallen from orange bottles, printed prescription
names of people who we had no relation.

I did not know then the difference in sound
between scattered pills and a tiny splash

or an empty room from the downtown lights—
we could not tell the people from monsters

my *Baby* from my *Bobby*, powder from poise.

The fever broke—or maybe it faded,
and the party carried on without us.

We knew then the legs weren't sad,
it was all that they had to carry.

The Grief

Plane crash, ejected from seat—it feels dug out
or plowed over, the way the fields in Indiana
look impossibly perfect, how someone must
spend their whole neurotic life in that field
snipping the blades of grass with shears.
I never want to sit in the emergency exit
seats because I wouldn't know how to direct
passengers off this disaster. I'd strap my floatation
device to the one absolute wrong place and go
down with the accidental plunge. You must
figure out your oxygen mask first before helping
others. I imagine us all fumbling, my cabin mates
watching me gasp as I freeze in panic. Most of it
is a response to panic, a fear that a loss
might detonate a bomb inside, jog loose the hot
pieces of my demise. What might explode out
the stability of my routine, what quakes and
disintegrates in its wake. Sometimes I scream
for no good reason other than release. With this,
there is none. I could scream and scream and still
not reach satisfaction. I am powerless in its trajectory.
My brother is so obsessed with Pangea in a literal sense—
he wants the terrain to be one, for the people he loves
to be less scattered, less separated. He literally thinks
pushing the continents together would make his family
whole. I understand the literal bits of it. The hole grief
leaves and the impulse to push the edges back, cover
the loss. At first, I joke that I grieve in reverse, that I am so
accepting, and my acceptance is denial. I am a collage
of the grieving process. I end on anger and will end there
so long as I live on this earth. I never think of the plane
crashing over water. It's always on land and everyone dies,
even after delegating emergency evacuation responsibilities
to a tight-lipped mother or distracted businessman.
That's the thing: there's no preparation for this. Everyone dies

eventually and we're still blown apart when it happens.
The continents are still shrouded, wet with coast and longing,
and even if we plummeted to water and paddled to land
it would never be the same. We mourn the loss, the change
and the crevices between this shift that dictate what we must
continue despite the uncontrollable loose screws spilling
from our once stable machines, washing up on mysterious shores.

Every Origin

How are you so attractive to everyone around you?
Never did figure this out myself, but want to.

I've had more partners than you
which shows not much is needed
to forge romance. You need two
willing participants. That's first.
Wherever you rummage them.

There's the banter electrified with endgame,
yes, language must make its bidding
before hands. Sometimes what's said
isn't anything to believe in.
Belief can do as little as slowly drip,
a leaky faucet.

Even when you know it's not worth pursuing,
it fills the time. Expands in a gap of slippage.
Sea monkeys grow where dead waters
stirred. Throw a feeling and see what sticks.

I used to take home a lot of losers
with winning at the forefront.
I'm not charming, it's obvious
by me telling you this. But I am warmed,

radiated. Charmed by the way
you fumble with dress zippers,
let eyelashes scoop my cheeks.

In my fantasy, you were naive
in love, adorably inexperienced.
Not once married. In my fantasy,
I strike the match that sets you
ablaze. I know it's self-absorbed
to want that. But in this delusion,

I take you too, immersed deep. I took a chance
on this mess. Swung it recklessly,
an anvil tied to a chain. Russian roulette
that I've gotten so good at, I can feel where the bullet is
in the revolver. For a while, I wanted to die, dragging you

into a house of unlucky cards. Blame the deck,
a reckless current inside me texting, assuming
you wouldn't text back.

You left when it was snowing. I felt relief
in a quiet sadness. Called Emily. There's the shift
from a confession, losing my interlocutors.
I don't want to get too sentimental,
but it wasn't until I saw you stranger than me
that I knew I must spin this barrel, holster the gun.

What did I love?
Your sadness. Not that you were
sad but that you knew its palpability.

Attraction felt harder to pinpoint,
uneasy and shipwrecked. Tomorrow
you could fuck another and feel it
better. I crave the inherent end.

But we keep firing this gun, surviving. I continue
to feel your whole burn. My body glows
in your brilliance. I blush. We never wither.
I am consistently surprised by how much
love pours out, not knowing what to call it,
or if its abundance will run dry. The body
always makes more until it bleeds out.

But this is regeneration, an amalgamation. Fantasy
and reality—a Venn diagram of what I want
and what I didn't think I could have, meeting
in the middle of a slivered eye shape:
what I want that I also have.

Here always like an apparition, a comforting smell.
I am not the internal arsonist I once was.
What can I owe it to? When did you begin
to love me despite myself? I've always leapt
without thinking about landing, let alone sticking it.

I don't think we ever have to land. Let's soar like
we are comprised of flotation devices in the biggest pool
of water we can find. You are moving muscles next to me,
a synchronized swimmer in the adjacent lane.
I mimic your moves, insert my own—we go back and forth
forever. Say you'll swim laps until it burns. Say this burning
is what keeps the whirlpool pulling us together. Let me
recreate forever with you. I have faith in firing the gun
pressed against my temple. You blow my brains

but not like that. Not today.
I didn't know I was a room
until you walked inside.
Instead of a vault,
I became a safe.
A keeper of secrets
instead of a spiller.
A spoiler. My darkness
always surrounds,
chocolate trophies melting
in the August sun. My bedroom
was a graveyard for nascent romances.
A flowerbed of tangled weeds. Wiry dime-
a-dozen. Everyone is so attracted to you.
You're the gun with one bullet. So blow me apart.

Say the tulips will creep out of me in the Spring.
Say it's eternal. I am forever a gardener to this.
I will grow the flowers if you bring the seeds.
I'll water and tend to it, promise to flourish
in spite of the perilous and strangling weeds.
There's so much soil to dig but I promise
to live as long as whatever we cultivate.

For Ivan Who Dreams of Elsewhere

Green beer bottle, clear mason jar.
So much broken glass in the streets,
I could make a mosaic of this place.

Touch it. I am not afraid
of anything. Not blood or disease.

All these shards make something
I only know in fragments.

Empty packs of Parliament Lights
and rat carcass with blood burst on the fur.
Useless wires languish on their poles.

Can I call you during the dark hour of telethon?
Look up, no one has a landline anymore.

You'll have to reply across cold train tracks—
trains sleep in the yard at night. Not like us.

You can be my son if I never have to
be your mother. Never have to miss you
when you grow into something else.

Never have to tell you: this world will try
to eat you and leave lacerations from dirty teeth.

I'll stitch your gashes, kiss the bandage
but do not attach yourself to me.
I am attached to terrible things.

I only live to tell you: *We are connected.*
We are golden somehow although

the meteorologists name
hurricanes after us.

I break into the dormant vehicles
resting in the lot and pretend

I steer the wheel of the galaxy that brought us together here.

I am the captain of disturbed dreams,
vinegar that drips from a broken jar.

Here is a lullaby for you about a dream a train had.

I sing *Run off your course!* while your eyes are shut.
Run off course! I yell it toward the arboretum.

I've made a wreath of cigarette butts for your door.
Hang it to welcome those who come over. Let it

welcome every new breath. Exhale all the waste.

Look around you, darling. It's trash day.

Notes

This entire collection is inspired deeply by *69 Love Songs* by the Magnetic Fields and *A Lover's Discourse* by Roland Barthes. Below, I tried to track as much as possible specifically where the references come from, but their words, thoughts, sounds, and poetry are threaded throughout that it would be nearly impossible for me to pin it all down.

"All of Us Are Disappearing All the Time": Big thanks to Stephen Young for the title.

"Rock Salt": Big thanks to the Pantone paint samples and Home Depot for the entryway into this poem.

"All the Flotsam and Jetsam of Hairdo": The title is a line in the poem "inside gertrude stein" by Lynn Emanuel.

"Pleasure Banquet": This entire poem is inspired by and borrows language from the section *Special Days* (fête/ festivity) in *A Lover's Discourse* by Roland Barthes.

"Beard Island, Population 1": The first line riffs off Magritte's "This is Not a Pipe," of course.

"Shatter": This was inspired by *69 Love Songs* by the Magnetic Fields, particularly "I Shatter."

"The World is My Rival": This entire poem is inspired by and borrows language from *A Lover's Discourse* by Roland Barthes, particularly the section titled *The Orange* (facheux / irksome).

"Absolutely Cuckoo": The poem is inspired by the Magnetic Fields song with the same title on *69 Love Songs*.

"the lover's discourse is today of an extreme solitude": The title is a direct quote from in *A Lover's Discourse* by Roland Barthes. I still can't remember or track down the William Carlos William poem that's referenced. I'm convinced I might've dreamed it...

"Burden of Desire" Borrows language and inspiration from the poem "The Sunlight" by Miguel Murphy.

"Majestic Blues": This poem started out titled "Pantone 292" as a tribute to the Magnetic Fields song on *69 Love Songs*, "Reno Dakota." The line: *Don't play fast & loose with me* is a play on the lyric "Do not play fast and loose with my heart." This poem also incorporates paint sample names per an exercise the poet Daniela Olszewska tweeted about.

"Parades go by": This also takes its title from the Magnetic Fields' *69 Love Songs*. *The most merciful thing in the world is the inability of the human mind to correlate all its contents* is a famous quote attributed to H.P. Lovecraft who was born in Providence, RI.

"When the world is trampling your safety": plays with language from the Shakespearian sonnet "To me, fair friend, you never can be old (Sonnet 104)."

"Through the Whale": This poem was inspired by Pablo Medina's "At the Blue Note" from his collection *The Man Who Wrote on Water.*

"Punk Love": Named after the Magnetic Fields song off *69 Love Songs*, this poem wouldn't exist without *Punk Rock Love* by Aaron Cometbus.

"I Think I Spider": The title is an English translation of a German idiom. I'm not confident I know what it means.

"What does heart mean? To have courage. To love.": This is a direct quote from *A Lover's Discourse* by Roland Barthes.

"Pity Us Poor Devils": I was sworn to secrecy about who designed this prompt but there were various "writing rules" and restrictions used to build this poem. The line *"I pity poor devils who have no experience of you and are dazzled by your radiance"* is from a Horace sonnet.

"you leave the room all at once": I attributed this in my notes to one of Andy Peterson's poems from *Anonymous Bouquet*, but after reading, re-reading, and asking Andy where the hell this line came from, we're still coming up empty. I believe truly that fragments of this poem are in that book somewhere, and I wanted to give proper thanks.

"THAT MAKES YOU SO EASY NOBODY AFTER": Andy Peterson sent me an image of German idioms translated into English as a prompt to write a poem. I chose "THAT MAKES YOU SO EASY NOBODY AFTER" because, to this day, I still have no idea what it's supposed to mean, even after some light research.

"Selfie at 29": Borrowed energy and inspiration from the poem "Self-Portrait at 28" by David Berman.

"The Triangle": This poem borrows deeply from *A Lover's Discourse* by Roland Barthes (particularly *Connivance* (connivence / connivance) and René Girard's work on Triangular Desire.

"Chill": If you want to know the inspiration for this poem, google "water hammer."

"Hexes & Curses": This poem was written after the poem "Curse Two: The Naming" by Cynthia Huntington.

"Bones of our assembly": I couldn't have done this without Andrew K. Peterson.

"With Change Machine and Pearls": This ekphrastic poem is in conversation with the image "Self-portrait with change machine" by Emma Bee Bernstein.

"The cactus where a heart should be": Another Magnetic Fields poem with a title from *69 Love Songs*. It is also inspired by the section *The Heart* (coeur / heart) in *A Lover's Discourse* by Roland Barthes.

"Horses Can't Swim": This ekphrastic poem was inspired by photographs of Jane's Carousel in Brooklyn underwater during Hurricane Sandy.

"je me souviens": The Quebec license plates say "je me souviens," literally translated to "I remember…" which was funny to me when I visited Montreal and I had no cell service—to get around, I had to study the map while I had Wi-Fi at the Airbnb or Tim Horton's down the street and remember the cross-streets, write down the addresses, and try to recall my spotty inventory of French vocabulary words to ask for help and to read the street signs about parking.

"From a supermarket": This poem is dedicated to the Price Chopper in downtown Storrs, Connecticut, my favorite writing spot on the UConn campus.

"Elegy": R.I.P. Whitney Houston.

"For Ivan Who Dreams of Elsewhere": This poem is dedicated to Ivan Cheung; Allston, Massachusetts; bad babies; boutique cupcake shops; and finally quitting your shitty job.

Love & Gratitude

My thank you must begin with the people who actually got it done—thank you Aurelia, Tod, and everyone at Spuyten Duyvil Press for believing in my voice and this manuscript. Ivan Cheung, thank you for spending time developing this original art piece for the cover and capturing its essence so succinctly, and also thank you for being such a wonderful friend. Stay golden.

Peter Shippy & John Skoyles, the early cultivators of this manuscript, thank you for being the best mentors a misfit like me could have. CAConrad, Darcie Dennigan, Elisa Gabbert: thank you immensely for your kind words about this book and for feeling its energy and embracing its life. To Emily Thomas, my derg, my ride or die & the most thoughtful, thorough reader of this manuscript early and often, over and over, and to Donald Vincent, otherwise known as Mr. Hip, for always shining, seeing the glitter around, and advocating for my work. You two make my student loan debt worth it.

I owe so much love and fist bumps to Andrew K. Peterson, Patrick Connolly, Sarah Torrey, Verrinia Amatulli, Janine Stankus, Sandra Simonds who challenged me to ask whoever the hell I want for blurbs and to not feel bad about it, Dominic Pettman for introducing me to *A Lover's Discourse* when I was a bratty undergrad at the New School, Jennifer Firestone for sparking the love of poetry inside of me, anyone who's ever hosted me at a reading, the poets, presses, and journals that inspire me (Jennifer L. Knox, Ada Limon, Maggie Nelson, Dean Young, Roxane Gay, Morgan Parker, Kaveh Akbar, Bloof Books, Birds LLC, Black Ocean, Wave, Tin House, Ploughshares, sixth finch, and on & on & on), and anyone who has ever been kind enough to help create and participate in a supportive poetry community. I see you and we need you. So much.

I have so much gratitude in my heart for the two companies I worked for during the course of writing and assembling this project—Hasbro, Inc. and Hallmark Cards, Inc., respectively. Without the flexibility, creativity, and support in my professional life, I would've never had the time, confidence, or commitment to get this done, and this is especially thanks to Forest Lee and Ally Rennell. Your encouragement meant/means more to me than you can know!

Of course my family, the Magnetic Fields, punk music, DIY literary journals, zines, the cities where these poems were born and born again (NYC, BOS, PVD, KCMO, et al.) and Jill Harrington for understanding who I am (and keeping me sane, these all kept me sane, except my family, ha ha ha), and last but not least, Chad Pope—thank you for lifting me up and existing as the big breath of fresh air away from the literary chaos. Your love motivated this book to become an actual object in the world to share rather than a disorganized folder on my computer, and there are no words to express a gratitude so deep. xo

CHARLOTTE SELEY is a poet and writer from the Hudson Valley region of New York, currently residing in Kansas City. *The World is My Rival* is her first full-length poetry collection. Find her on the web at charlotteseley.com.